BLEAT

A book of fun for goat lovers

Compiled by Bronwyn Eley

'The grass is always greener on the
other side of the fence.'

EVERY GOAT ON THE PLANET

There are two types of people in this world: those who want a pet goat, and those who do not. For the former, this book is for you.

There is something about animals that inspires the child within us all. Something that gets grown adults to lean against their car window and bleat like a goat, moo like a cow, or coo with delight at a field of adorable animals.

Goats have been valued for over 10,000 years and are the first suspected domesticated animal. Not to mention goat milk is the number-one consumed milk in the world. Speaking of things that milk goes with, did you know there's a legend that says goats discovered coffee? Legend has it that the goats of an Ethiopian goat herder munched on the berries of a certain unfamiliar tree. That night they were energetic and refused to sleep.

Yet one more reason to bow down to goats!

Whether it's the way their tiny tails wag, the stark frankness of their piercing gaze, or their manic attempts to get past any fence put in their way, goats have inspired obsession and adoration through the ages.

And don't even get us started on the adorable, hilarious yet concerning quirk of the *fainting goat*.

This book is a celebration of our love for this charismatic animal. With quotes from Sandra Bullock, Aristotle, Cicero and Jason Momoa, *Bleat* is designed to remind people of why we can't seem to get enough of those cute little faces.

Goat lovers everywhere, this book is for you. Just be sure not to leave it unattended anywhere near your goat … or they might eat it.

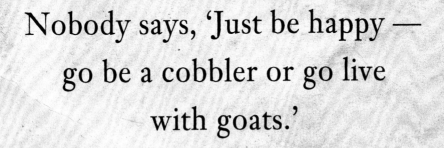

Nobody says, 'Just be happy —
go be a cobbler or go live
with goats.'

SANDRA BULLOCK

Every man can tell how many goats
or sheep he possesses, but not
how many friends.

MARCUS TULLIUS CICERO

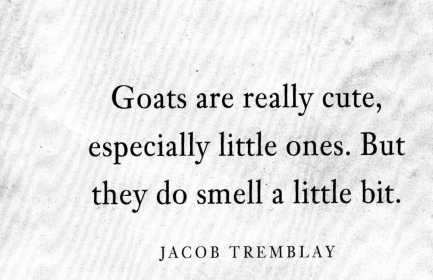

Goats are really cute,
especially little ones. But
they do smell a little bit.

JACOB TREMBLAY

The blood of a goat will
shatter a diamond.

ARISTOTLE

A close family member once
offered his opinion that I exhibit
the phone manners of a goat, then
promptly withdrew the charge —
out of fairness to goats.

JEFFREY KLUGER

I think that the reason why *Goats* is called *Goats* is because you can't give direction to goats. They do what they want. That's the point of this film.

GRAHAM PHILLIPS

A few months after the goats came,
I began jeering back at them.

JON KATZ

And I like pygmy goats,
because they're just lovely.

RICHARD HAMMOND

In Ethiopia … you might find a seven year old expected to take fifteen goats out into the fields for the whole day with only a chapati to eat and his whistle. Why are we so afraid to give our children responsibilities like this?

JOANNA LUMLEY

Where I live, there's a lot
of canyons. We're climbing
constantly — we're like
mountain goats. I'm just trying
to get better at that.

JOEY SANTIAGO

I've got kids, goats. My wife
always wanted a donkey, so
I bought her one.

JASON MOMOA

You Liberals think that
goats are just sheep from
broken homes.

MALCOLM BRADBURY

Books are no different from goats!
They enjoy an afternoon out
on the lawn.

KATE BERNHEIMER

He who has conquered doubt
and fear has conquered failure.

JAMES LANE ALLEN

When we were little, we used to play with the goats all the time. We each had our own little goat, and we'd go and run around with them.

JESSICA SPRINGSTEEN

I'm terrified of goats.

ANNALISE BASSO

An old goat is never the more
reverend for his beard.

THOMAS FULLER

Don't approach a goat from the front, a horse from the back, or a fool from any side.

JEWISH PROVERB

The only bit of wisdom he wanted
to share about them was this:
'Sheep eat low, goats eat high.'
This turned out to be so.

JON KATZ

Always stand on principle
even if you stand alone.

JOHN QUINCY ADAMS

Look carefully at the goat
sitting on the edge of the cliff:
Everything that shows you the
peace of being fearless is a great
teacher for you! That goat is a
teacher for you, respect him!

MEHMET MURAT ILDAN

The goat is a hardy animal,
and good health is the rule in
herds that are well managed.

VARIOUS

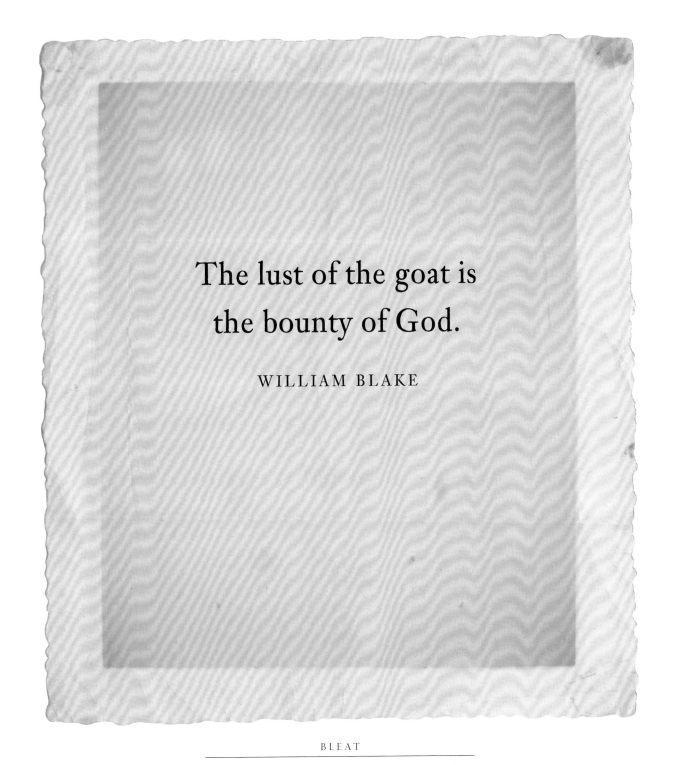

The lust of the goat is
the bounty of God.

WILLIAM BLAKE

One day I will rule the world
with a goat by my side!

JHONEN VASQUEZ

Well, only Japanese may understand it, but I'm like a goat or something that likes high places.

TAMAE WATANABE

He who lets the goat be laid
on his shoulders is soon after
forced to carry the cow.

ITALIAN PROVERB

Bring me coffee before
I turn into a goat!

JOHANN SEBASTIAN BACH

I want to go about like the
light-footed goats.

JOHANNA SPYRI

Happiness never decreases by being shared.

BUDDHA

The beginning is the most
important part of the work.

PLATO

In all things of nature there is something of the marvellous.

ARISTOTLE

If your actions inspire others to dream more, learn more, do more and become more, you are a leader.

JOHN QUINCY ADAMS

The world is not to be
divided into sheeps and goats.
Not all things are black nor
all things white.

ALFRED KINSEY

On second thought I think
I am crazier than my goat.

REMEDIOS VARO

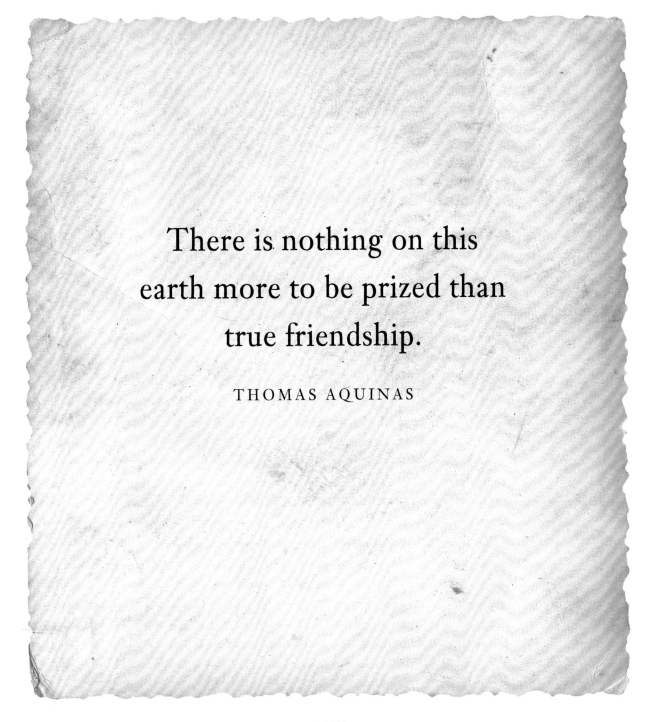

There is nothing on this earth more to be prized than true friendship.

THOMAS AQUINAS

He who fears being
conquered is sure of defeat.

NAPOLEON BONAPARTE

Do I not destroy my enemies
when I make them my friends?

ABRAHAM LINCOLN

Be yourself. Everyone else
is already taken.

OSCAR WILDE

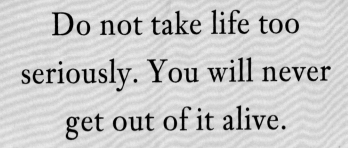

Do not take life too seriously. You will never get out of it alive.

ELBERT HUBBARD

Opportunity is missed by most
people because it is dressed in
overalls and looks like work.

THOMAS A. EDISON

As long as you live, keep
learning how to live.

SENECA

I've made my music so that it could be about anything and everybody — whether it's a guy, a female or a goat — and everybody can relate to that.

SAM SMITH

It's never too late to be what
you might have been.

GEORGE ELIOT

See all living beings as your
father or mother, and love
them as if you were their child.

ATISA

I never made it to the school choir because the music teacher didn't like my voice. I was pretty sad. But he was probably right, I did have a voice a bit like a goat but my dad told me to never give up and to keep going and it's paid off.

SHAKIRA

Whatever you are, be a good one.

ABRAHAM LINCOLN

You can't train a goat. You can't. You can't. So I don't recommend making a movie with a goat in a major role to anyone.

ROBERT EGGERS

I always thought it was a goat that kicked me over the fence. My mama told me the other day it was a cow. Now I'm sort of scared of both.

KELSEA BALLERINI

It don't take a genius to spot
a goat in a flock of sheep.

WILL ROGERS

What is a friend? A single soul dwelling in two bodies.

ARISTOTLE

I want to be like one of those little fainting goats that get scared and then just fall over. I want to go and go and then drop dead in the middle of something I'm loving to do. And if that doesn't happen, if I wind up sitting in a wheelchair, at least I'll have my high heels on.

DOLLY PARTON

I don't know how old I am
because a goat ate the Bible
that had my birth certificate
in it. The goat lived to be
twenty-seven.

SATCHEL PAIGE

There was never a moment in
my life that I remember not
being a crazy animal lover!

BETH OSTROSKY STERN

I am a mountain goat that keeps
going and going and going, I cannot
be stopped, I just keep going.

SEPP BLATTER

When I was eight years old, I wrote a paragraph-long short story about a goat on my mother's hundred-pound, black-and-white-screen laptop. The story came about largely because I liked the way the word 'goat' looked on the page, but I decided then and there that I wanted to be a writer. That desire never changed.

TEA OBREHT

This life of ours … human
life is like a flower gloriously
blooming in a meadow:
along comes a goat, eats it
up — no more flower.

ANTON CHEKHOV

Peace comes from within.
Do not seek it without.

BUDDHA

When we lose the right to be different, we lose the privilege to be free.

CHARLES EVANS HUGHES

Animals are such
agreeable friends — they
ask no questions, they
pass no criticisms.

GEORGE ELIOT

The fate of animals is of far
greater importance to me than
the fear of appearing ridiculous.

EMILE ZOLA

I've never met an animal I didn't like, and I can't say the same thing about people.

DORIS DAY

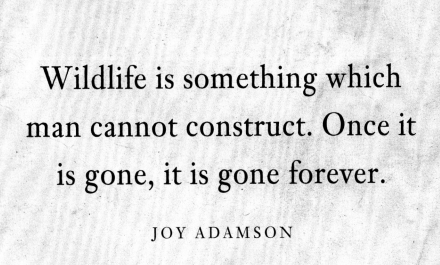

Wildlife is something which
man cannot construct. Once it
is gone, it is gone forever.

JOY ADAMSON

He who is brave is free.

SENECA

Goats are the cable talk show panellists of the animal world, ready at a moment's notice to interject, interrupt, and opine. They have something to say about everything, little of it complimentary. They are the most impertinent animals I have ever known.

JON KATZ

We can judge the heart
of a man by his treatment
of animals.

IMMANUEL KANT

Animals are the bridge
between us and the beauty
of all that is natural.

TRISHA MCCAGH

Animals share with us the
privilege of having a soul.

PYTHAGORAS

All of the animals except for man
know that the principle business
of life is to enjoy it.

SAMUEL BUTLER

An animal's eyes have
the power to speak a
great language.

MARTIN BUBER

Smile, it's free therapy.

DOUGLAS HORTON

Until one has loved an
animal, a part of one's soul
remains unawakened.

ANATOLE FRANCE

I think I could turn and live
with the animals, they are so
placid and self-contained.

WALT WHITMAN

Clearly, animals know more
than we think, and think a great
deal more than we know.

IRENE M. PEPPERBERG

The greatness of a nation and its moral progress can be judged by the way its animals are treated.

GANDHI

Each species is a masterpiece,
a creation assembled with
extreme care and genius.

E.O. WILSON

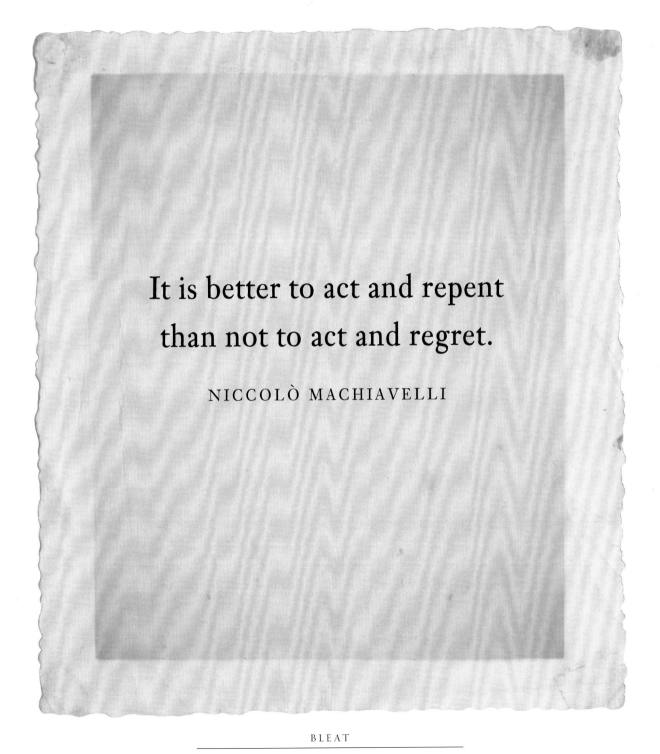

It is better to act and repent
than not to act and regret.

NICCOLÒ MACHIAVELLI

The love for all living creatures is
the most noble attribute of man.

CHARLES DARWIN

Also in the Animal Happiness series

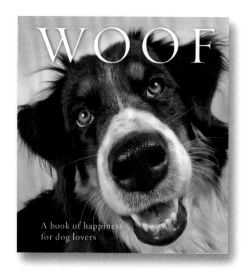

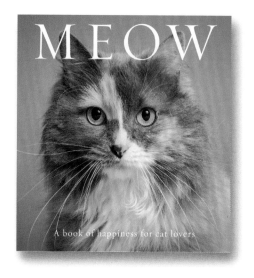

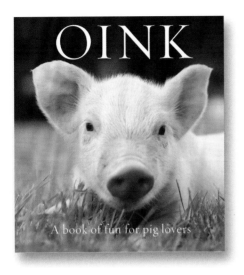

OINK

A book of fun for pig lovers

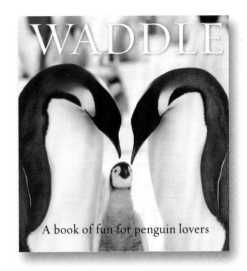

WADDLE

A book of fun for penguin lovers

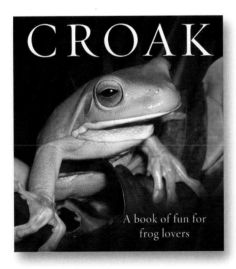

CROAK

A book of fun for frog lovers

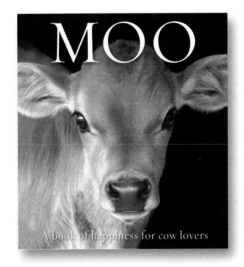

MOO

A book of happiness for cow lovers

First published 2022

Exisle Publishing Pty Ltd
PO Box 864, Chatswood, NSW 2057, Australia
226 High Street, Dunedin, 9016, New Zealand
www.exislepublishing.com

Copyright © 2022 in published work: Exisle Publishing Pty Ltd

A CiP record for this book is available from the
National Library of Australia.

ISBN 978 1 922539 29 8

Designed by Mark Thacker
Typeset in Archetype 24 on 36pt
Photographs courtesy of Shutterstock
Printed in China

This book uses paper sourced under ISO 14001 guidelines from
well-managed forests and other controlled sources.

2 4 6 8 10 9 7 5 3 1